The Largest Indoor Parks and Malls

Susan K. Mitchell
AR B.L.: 6.1
Points: 1.0   MG

MEGASTRUCTURES

THE LARGEST INDOOR PARKS AND MALLS

by Susan K. Mitchell

Gareth Stevens
Publishing

Please visit our web site at: www.garethstevens.com
For a free color catalog describing Gareth Stevens Publishing's
list of high-quality books, call 1-800-542-2595 (USA)
or 1-800-387-3178 (Canada).

Library of Congress Cataloging-in-Publication Data

Mitchell, Susan K.
    Largest indoor parks and malls / by Susan K. Mitchell.
       p. cm. — (Megastructures)
    Includes bibliographical references and index.
    ISBN-10: 0-8368-8362-4 (lib. bdg.)
    ISBN-13: 978-0-8368-8362-6 (lib. bdg.)
    1. Megastructures. 2. Commercial buildings. I. Title.
  NA9053.M43M58   2007
  725—dc22   2007012980

This edition first published in 2008 by
Gareth Stevens Publishing
A Weekly Reader® Company
1 Reader's Digest Road
Pleasantville, NY 10570-7000 USA

Editorial direction: Mark J. Sachner
Editor: Barbara Kiely Miller
Art direction and design: Tammy West
Picture research: Diane Laska-Swanke
Production: Jessica Yanke
Illustrations: Spectrum Creative Inc.

Picture credits: Cover, title © TWPhoto/CORBIS; pp. 5, 29 © Streeter
Lecka/Getty Images; pp. 7, 14, 17, 24, 27 © AP Images; p. 9 © Karen
Bleier/AFP/Getty Images; pp. 10-11 © Timo Gans/AFP/Getty Images;
p. 16 © Stephanie Kuykendal/CORBIS; p. 19 © Galen Rowell/CORBIS;
p. 20 © James Marshall/CORBIS

Printed in the United States of America

1 2 3 4 5 6 7 8 9 11 10 09 08 07

CONTENTS

On the Cover: Beachgoers soak up artifical sunlight on the indoor beach at Seagaia Resort's Ocean Dome in Japan.

CHAPTER 1

THE GREAT INDOORS

In the great outdoors, people climb rocks. They race down snowy slopes. Many people love simply lying on the beach. All of these are fun outdoor activities. Even visits to amusement parks and zoos are open-air events. All outdoor adventures can come to a stop, however, when the weather changes.

Today, some creative architects have found a way around bad weather. They have constructed huge buildings all over the world where people can enjoy outdoor activities year-round — by staying indoors! Although the sizes of the buildings are amazing, what is inside makes them truly different. Special systems inside these indoor parks and malls recreate the outside world. Making the indoors look like the outdoors takes lots of planning and design.

A designer must keep temperature, air, and lighting in mind when creating an artificial outdoor environment inside a building. Special systems and machines can create snow or waves of water. Some systems even create artificial skies. They use lights to create sunrises and sunsets as well as bright blue daytime and starlit night skies.

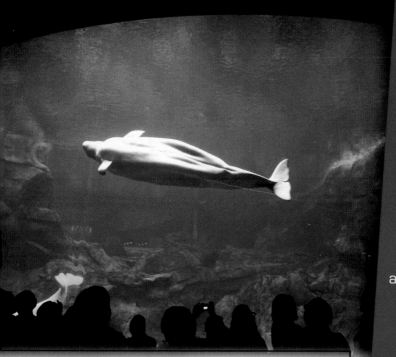

This enormous Beluga whale is just one of the many huge underwater animals that call the Georgia Aquarium home.

See the Sea Up Close

At the Georgia Aquarium in Atlanta, visitors can experience walking through the ocean. With more than 450,000 square feet (41,800 square meters) of space, the aquarium is the world's largest. The building was built around its huge, super-thick acrylic windows, not the reverse. Acrylic is a super-strong clear plastic. More than twelve thousand acrylic windows were used throughout the aquarium.

The windows for the holding tanks were built in Japan. The window panels were formed from many layers of acrylic. Each panel took months to complete.

The largest panel of acrylic windows is 61 feet (19 meters) wide. It is 23 feet (7 m) tall and 2 feet (.6 m) thick. This enormous window allows people to peer eye-to-eye at the biggest fish in the world. The aquarium is the only facility in the country to house whale sharks!

Inside Nature

The Henry Doorly Zoo in Omaha, Nebraska, has taken going to the zoo to a new level. The zoo has recreated some of the biggest ecosystems in the world and brought them indoors. One of those ecosystems, the Lied Jungle (pronounced LEED) is the world's largest indoor rain forest. First opened in April 1992, it stretches across more than one acre (one-half hectare) of land. While the exhibit is small in comparison to a real rain forest, it reaches more than 80 feet (24 m) toward the clear roof. The tallest trees are as tall as an eight-story building!

Nebraska architect Stanley J. How had already designed several other exhibits for the Henry Doorly Zoo when he was put in charge of designing this unique indoor space. He made the roof of the rain forest building out of special reinforced plastic around a metal frame. The plastic lets plenty of sunlight inside the rain forest structure. Much of this indoor rain forest is also manmade. Rocky areas and big trees were constructed from metal frames that are covered with fiberglass and cement. The rest of the lush plants in the Lied Jungle, however, are real.

Controlling the environment inside the Lied Jungle is important. If the temperature and humidity, or moisture in the air, are not kept at a certain level, the many different plants and animals could suffer. To make the building seem more like a real rain forest, a special air system had to be designed. A rain forest is hot and humid all year, not at all like Nebraksa's normal weather. Zoo officials hired Control Services Inc. to create an air system for the Lied Jungle.

MEGA FACTS

The Lied Jungle's building houses several waterfalls. The largest is 50 feet (15 m) tall. It is the second tallest waterfall in Nebraska.

In addition to the Lied Jungle, the Henry Doorly Zoo can also boast of having the largest indoor desert in its Desert Dome.

"We wanted to simulate actual rainforest conditions by producing [high] humidity during the day, followed by cool building temperatures at night," explains Chuck Kopocis, the vice-president of Control Services. The result is an amazing recreation of an actual rain forest in the heart of the midwestern United States.

CHAPTER 2

MALL SPRAWL

An all-day shopping trip is a favorite activity for many people around the world. A shopping mall gives people a place to shop, eat, or be entertained all under one roof. The Mall of America in Bloomington, Minnesota, is one of the largest mega-malls in the world. It is definitely the largest single mall in the United States.

The massive Mall of America sits on a giant piece of land that once held Metropolitan Stadium. When a new stadium was built in 1982 about 12 miles (19 kilometers) away in Minneapolis, the land was left empty. The town of Bloomington came up with several plans for the land. The Ghermezian brothers were finally hired to develop the land into a giant mall.

The Ghermezian brothers are land developers from Canada. With their company, Triple Five Group, they designed a mall where people could do more than just shop. They had already designed another of the world's largest malls in Edmonton, Canada.

Construction of the 4.2 million square foot (390,000 sq m) mall began in 1989. It opened on August 11, 1992. The outside of the Mall of America is not particularly amazing. It is a basic rectangular, four-story building. It is the sheer size of the mall that is

The Mall of America often showcases unusual exhibits like these replicas of the International Space Station, a Space Shuttle, and astronauts, all made entirely of Legos™.

 MEGA FACTS

Mall walking is a popular form of exercise for many people. The walking distance around one level of the Mall of America is more than half a mile (1 km).

The Great Malls of China

The world's largest shopping mall is the South China Mall in Dongguan, China. It opened in late 2005. In fact, China can boast of having four of the top ten largest malls in the world. Several other large malls are already being built in China, however, that will eclipse the size of the South China Mall.

With more than 7 million square feet (660,000 sq m) of space, the South China Mall is divided into seven zones that look like different places around the world. One area looks like the watery canals of Venice, Italy. Another area resembles California. Others are modeled to look like Paris, Amsterdam, Egypt, Rome, and the Caribbean.

outstanding. Officials at the mall estimate that seven Yankee Stadiums or thirty-two Boeing 747 airplanes could fit inside it!

What really sets this mall apart from other shopping malls is what is inside the huge building. It has the usual mall attractions, just more of them. There are more than 500 stores, a 14-screen movie theater, and more than 50 different restaurants.

It also has attractions, however, not found in most shopping malls.

College and high school classes are held in areas of the mall. The Mall of America even has a bank and a wedding chapel. Under the mall roof, there is a 1.2-million-gallon (4.5-million-liter) aquarium, museums, and a church. It also has a huge amusement park called The Park at MOA. All of this fits inside one gigantic building!

The Timberland Twister is a roller coaster with spinning cars. Located at The Park at MOA, it is one of the first of its kind.

In the operation of an indoor park or mall, providing security on a grand scale can be more important than artificial air or lighting systems. The massive size of these structures creates an even greater need for state-of-the-art security. The Mall of America has a highly trained staff of more than one hundred security officers. They are stationed all over the mega-mall.

More than 160 cameras are located throughout the mall, the amusement park, and all the parking areas. In addition, mall designers installed 130 call boxes in the mall. In emergency situations, visitors may use more than 100 pay phones.

11

Bigger and Better

There are current plans to make the Mall of America even bigger. The expansion would be built on 42 acres (17 hectares) of land and connected to the north side of the mall. The Ghermezian brothers who designed the current mall are leading the project.

The plans include an indoor golf course and water park. An indoor ice skating rink large enough for a National Hockey League (NHL) team is also planned. "When the expansion is completed," said Nader Ghermezian, "people … will have access to the number one tourist attraction in the United States."

MEGA FACTS

If a shopper spent ten minutes in each store at the Mall of America, it would take that person three and a half days to go through the entire mall.

CHAPTER 3

SKIING THE SANDS

Without snow, skiing is impossible. Many parts of the world never become cold enough for snow or skiing, however. Cold mountain areas like Colorado or parts of Europe have lots of popular ski resorts. The last place anyone would think of if they want to speed down a snowy slope, however, would be the deserts of Dubai.

Temperatures in Dubai can soar to more than 100 °Fahrenheit (38 °Celsius) under the desert sun. Dubai is an emirate, or territory, in the United Arab Emirates (UAE), near Saudi Arabia in the Middle East. People living in Dubai are more accustomed to sand than snow. At Ski Dubai, however, architecture and technology have combined to bring snow indoors.

Defying Mother Nature

Opened in September 2005, Ski Dubai is part of the giant Mall of the Emirates in Dubai. In 2003, owners of the mall hired amusement park design company Thinkwell Design & Production to create the indoor ski resort. Other countries, like Germany and the Netherlands, already had similar indoor ski parks that were even larger.

The natural climate of those countries, however, was nothing close to the hot, dusty climate of Dubai. The idea

The general manager of Ski Dubai (*in front with back turned*) watches over the man-made winter wonderland as snow is being made.

of bringing snow to such a hot climate seemed crazy. "We like crazy ideas," said Craig Hanna, the chief creative officer of Thinkwell Design & Production, in an interview with a Los Angeles newspaper.

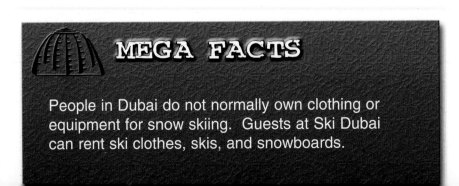

MEGA FACTS

People in Dubai do not normally own clothing or equipment for snow skiing. Guests at Ski Dubai can rent ski clothes, skis, and snowboards.

What the designers created was a 242,000-square-foot (22,500-sq-m) winter wonderland. Ski Dubai looks like any outdoor ski resort — if you don't count the windows and walls! Ski lifts carry skiers high above the snow to the top of each slope. There are five ski slopes at different levels of difficulty. The tallest slope is twenty-five stories tall! Skiers race 1,320 feet (402 m) to the bottom of the slope.

Reality Lift Ticket

Not everyone is ready or willing to fling themselves down a mountain of snow. For those visitors, Hanna designed a 30,000-square-foot (2,787-sq-m) snow park. Craig Hanna took creating the artificial "reality" very seriously. He studied natural snowy landscapes on trips to Mount Baldy in Southern California.

He and the other designers maintained a sense of adventure, however. They made sure to include an ice

The slopes at Ski Dubai might be manmade, but the snow is very real. To create the snow, super-cooled water is sent to machines throughout Ski Dubai. Tiny particles of the chilled water are shot into the air above the ski slopes. When the particles of cold water hit the freezing temperatures inside the building, they crystallize and form snow.

This snowmaking process is the same one used by outdoor ski resorts to add extra snow to mountain slopes. Each night, the temperature in Ski Dubai is lowered from 28 °F (-2 °C) to 19 °F (-7 °C). The snow-making machines work to create 30 tons (27 tonnes) of fresh snow each night.

Visitors to Ski Dubai can race each other down its twin bobsled tracks.

MEGA FACTS

Dubai is the only emirate that does not rely on money from oil production. Tourism is Dubai's main source of income.

cave, toboggan slides, and a snowball shooting gallery. The ice cave is kept much colder than the rest of the already chilly Ski Dubai.

Located under one of the slopes, the ice cave is kept at 19 °F (-7 °C). In the middle of the cave is a huge ice sculpture of a dragon. Programmed lights sparkle off ice crystals covering the cave walls. The ice cave is just one of many places at Ski Dubai where the real meets the artificial to create a uniquely manmade experience.

It would be difficult to guess that a snowy ski resort lies inside the sloped metal exterior of Ski Dubai.

Moving Mountains

Snow skiing is not the only mountain activity that has moved inside a building. Indoor rock climbing has become very popular in recent years. Visitors to these climbing facilities can test their strength without the danger of serious injury or death.

One of the largest indoor rock climbing gyms in the world is Carabiner's Climbing Gym in New Bedford, Massachusetts. The warehouse-sized building covers 32,600 square feet (3,029 sq m) of space. Its highest rock wall is 65 feet (20 m) tall. The gym includes rock walls of different heights and sizes so people of various ages and abilities can enjoy climbing them.

The rock walls are usually made of wood over a metal framework. Hard plastic foot and finger holds are bolted all over the wall. They can be moved to create different routes for climbers.

CHAPTER 4

OUT OF THIS WORLD AMUSEMENT

In most amusement parks, rain can put roller coaster rides on hold. Rain has no power, however, over the roller coasters in the world's largest indoor amusement park. Located in the West Edmonton Mall in Canada, Galaxyland is a theme park with a roof.

The West Edmonton Mall was once the largest mall in the world. Designed by the Ghermezian brothers, Phase I of the mall opened in September 1981. Its shopping area covered more than 1 million square feet (93,000 sq m). At that time, the amusement park was called Fantasyland and had only a few children's rides.

In 1983, Phase II was completed and the amusement park area became a fully developed theme park, complete with a few roller coasters. By then, the West Edmonton Mall had added another million square feet. It had more than 450 stores. The mall had an enormous ice-skating rink, too.

Big Enough to Bend Your Mind

Phase III of the West Edmonton Mall was completed in 1985. By now, the mall was a gigantic 5 million square feet (464,500 sq m)! That same year, the Mindbender roller coaster was added to the mall's amusement park.

The indoor lake where a replica of the *Santa Maria* is docked is also home to trained sea lions and other ocean animals.

 MEGA FACTS

Inside the West Edmonton Mall, there is a full-sized replica of one of Christopher Columbus's ships – the *Santa Maria*. It sits in a 20-foot- (6-m-) deep, manmade lake in the mall.

Makers of the Ultimate Mall Experience

The Ghermezian brothers are pioneers at transforming a shopping mall into a complete entertainment experience. The four brothers immigrated to Canada from Iran in the 1960s. They came with their father, Jacob Ghermezian. Since then, they have developed some of the largest malls in the world.

The brothers are secretive and rarely seen together in public. Nader is the family spokesperson. He handles much of the public negotiations and interviews. Eskander is the construction expert. Rafael handles financial matters, and Bahman runs business operations. The family has been honored by the Canadian government for creating huge numbers of jobs by building their mega-malls in both Canada and the United States.

In 2005, the popular submarine rides (*above*) at West Edmonton Mall were replaced with a Deep Sea Derby bumper boat ride.

Even today, the Mindbender is the world's tallest and longest indoor roller coaster.

The Mindbender is 136 feet (41 m) tall and hits a top speed of 60 miles (97 km) per hour. Riders are whipped around 4,198 feet (1280 m) of steel track. The Mindbender is also the only triple-looped indoor roller coaster in the world.

In the early 1990s, officials at Disneyland in California filed suit against the Ghermezian brothers and the West Edmonton Mall. They claimed the Fantasyland name belonged to the Walt Disney Company. After a long court battle, a judge agreed. In 1995, owners of the West Edmonton

MEGA FACTS

The Space Shot at Galaxyland is the world's tallest indoor tower ride. It launches riders 120 feet (37 m) into the air and then lets them freefall back to the ground.

Tragedy Strikes!

One of the worst roller coaster accidents in history happened on the Mindbender in 1986. As riders sped through the track's second loop, loose bolts caused the wheels of the last train car to come off. The back of the train began to whip back and forth. Several passengers were thrown from the cars.

The train did not have enough speed to complete the third loop. It stopped in mid-loop and began to race backwards. The cars crashed into a concrete support post. Three people died in the accident.

The Mindbender was shut down. Coaster designers blamed Galaxyland officials for poor inspections and maintenance. Investigators also blamed the accident on the ride's wheel design. Since then, the Mindbender was redesigned. Safety and inspection practices were greatly increased. No other accidents have occurred.

Mall were forced to change the name of Fantasyland to Galaxyland.

Along with a new name came a new space-age theme. Today, Galaxyland has twenty-four rides. Eight of them are for beginners. Seven are advanced, hair-raising thrill rides. Nine others fall somewhere in the middle on the thrill scale. New rides are also being added as the theme park expands along with the mall.

MEGA FACTS

Beginning in 2007, a new ride at Galaxyland will wind its way around the entire amusement park. The individual cars will spin as they race around the track.

CHAPTER 5

CONQUERING THE SEA

There is no end to the beaches in the island country of Japan. The city of Miyazaki on the Japanese island of Kyushu has long been known for great surfing. So then why does Miyazaki also have one of the largest indoor beaches and water parks in the world?

Miyazaki usually has toasty temperatures and clean, clear water along its beaches. The beaches in Japan, however, also have to deal with less than ideal surfing weather during part of the year — typhoon season. Typhoons are giant storms similar to hurricanes. They have high winds and huge waves. Typhoons occur fairly often in Japan. The same great waves that provide excellent surfing can destroy towns during a typhoon.

Surfing Inside

In 1993, the Seagaia Resort in Miyazaki opened the Ocean Dome, an indoor beach where weather is not a factor. The resort is not very far inland from Miyazaki's natural beaches. While not even the Ocean Dome can take on a typhoon, it does provide for year-round beach fun in less than ideal weather. The Ocean Dome is one of the largest indoor water parks in the world. It was designed by Japanese company Mitsubishi Heavy Industrial Group (MHI).

Weather-proof Water Parks

Wisconsin Dells, Wisconsin, is a city full of water parks. It has more water parks than anywhere else in the United States. The Dells is also home to the biggest indoor water park — the Kalahari Waterpark. The Kalahari covers 125,000 square feet (11,600 sq m). This indoor park is full of enormous water slides and a huge wave pool.

The Kalahari Resorts company owns another indoor water park in Sandusky, Ohio. By the fall of 2007, it will be expanded from 80,000 square feet (7,432 sq m) to 173,000 square feet (16,072 sq m). After the expansion, the Kalahari park in Sandusky will officially become the largest indoor water park in the United States.

Even when the Ocean Dome's retractable roof is closed (*above*), its translucent panels let the blue sky shine through.

The huge Ocean Dome is more than 900 feet (275 m) long and 300 feet (90 m) wide. It covers 322,752 square feet (29,985 sq m). The Ocean Dome can hold 13,500 gallons (51,100 liters) of manmade salt water. The temperature inside this indoor paradise is kept at a constant 86 °F (30 °C). Covering the huge building is one of the largest retractable domed roofs in the world.

WATER PARK SLIDE

STAIRS

SLIDE

WATER PUMP

WATER FILTER

POOL

KEY
→ FLOW OF WATER

Thousands of gallons (liters) of water are pumped through water park slides each day to give visitors a wild, wet ride. The arrows show the direction of the water through a slide.

The Biggest Beach

Germany is not a place where anyone would expect to find a tropical island. The weather in the European country is often very cold and snowy. Near Berlin, Germany, however, is the largest indoor water park in the world. At more than 700,000 square feet (65,030 sq m), the Tropical Islands water park is also one of the largest freestanding buildings in the world.

The park opened in 2004. It is located in what used to be a giant aircraft hanger built to house huge gas-filled zeppelins, or blimps. The domed Tropical Islands water park is tall enough to hold the Statue of Liberty. It is long enough to hold the Eiffel Tower laid on its side.

The retractable roof is made up of four independent arched panels. The hard, translucent panels are stretched over an enormous steel frame. The roof can be opened in less than ten minutes. It is only opened, however, when the weather outside matches the controlled weather conditions inside the dome.

Making Waves

MHI also designed an amazing system that creates waves from 6 feet (2 m) to 10 feet (3 m) tall inside the Ocean Dome. Giant hydraulic pumps are hidden behind a 230-foot- (70-m-) back wall along the fake ocean. The water along this wall is 10 feet (3 m) deep. Twenty large pumps suck up huge amounts of water into a storage tank.

The water is then forced back downward into the pool at high speeds. When the flush of water hits the bottom of the Ocean Dome pool, it rolls back toward the surface into a surfable wave. More than 1,800 tons (1,633 tonnes) of water are needed to create each wave.

Five different water release sections are arranged along the back of the Ocean Dome. Water can be released through different sections to create a variety of waves. The size, shape, and direction of each wave can be

MEGA FACTS

A giant artificial volcano inside the Ocean Dome "erupts" every thirty minutes when the waves start rolling.

This aerial view shows the **Ocean Dome** on a rare day when the roof is open, letting in natural sun.

controlled by the water-pumping system. The wave system, like all other nature simulation systems, helps bring a piece of nature to the great indoors.

MEGA FACTS

The Ocean Dome cost 200 billion Japanese Yen — or about 2 billion U.S. dollars — to build! The water park has not earned its construction cost back yet.

1981 Phase I of the West Edmonton Mall opens.

1983 Phase II of the West Edmonton Mall opens. Fantasyland adds roller coasters.

1985 The Mindbender roller coaster opens. Fantasyland becomes the largest indoor amusement park in the world.

1986 Tragic crash of the Mindbender roller coaster. The ride is shut down for redesigning.

1992 Lied Jungle exhibit opens. It becomes the largest indoor rainforest in the world.

The Mall of America opens. It becomes the largest indoor mall in the United States.

1993 Seagaia Ocean Dome opens in Japan.

1995 Fantasyland changes its name to Galaxyland.

2004 Tropical Island opens in Germany. It becomes the world's largest indoor water park.

2005 South China Mall opens. It becomes the largest indoor mall in the world.

Ski Dubai indoor ski park opens.

GLOSSARY

artificial — not natural; manmade

climate — the weather conditions in a certain area

ecosystems — a variety of living things and the environment in which they live

emirate — a territory or nation ruled by an Emir, or Middle Eastern royalty. There are seven separate emirates, including Dubai, in the United Arab Emirates.

expansion — an increase in something's size

fiberglass — glass in the form of fibers that are then used to make other materials

humidity — the amount of water vapor in the air

hydraulic — operated by pressurized water or other liquids

immigrated — having arrived in a new country to live

particles — very small pieces or amounts

reinforced — made stronger by the use of additional material, assistance, or support

replica — an exact copy of an item

retractable — able to be drawn or pulled back and opened

tourism — the business of providing services to people traveling for pleasure

translucent — allowing light to pass through, yet not completely clear

zeppelins — also called blimps; large, gas filled airships

TO FIND OUT MORE

Books

Building Big. David Macaulay (Houghton Mifflin)

Minnesota. The United States (series). Julie Murray (ABDO Press)

Video

Extreme Engineering: Dubai Ski Resort (Discovery Channel) NR

Web Sites

Building Big — Bridges, Domes, Skyscrapers, Dams, Tunnels
www.pbs.org/wgbh/buildingbig/index.html
This interactive site looks at the materials and methods used
to build big structures.

Georgia Aquarium
www.georgiaaquarium.org/kidscorner
Read about the animals and exhibits at this huge aquarium.

Ski Dubai
www.skidxb.com/English/default.aspx
English language version of Ski Dubai website

Galaxyland
www.westedmall.com/play/galaxyland.asp
Web site of the West Edmonton Mall

Ocean Dome
www.seagaia.co.jp/english/od/od.html
Official Web site of the Seagaia resort

INDEX

About the Author

Susan K. Mitchell lives near Houston, Texas, and is actually more a fan of the great outdoors. She is a teacher and author of several children's picture books. Susan has also written many non-fiction chapter books for kids. She has a wonderful husband, two daughters, a dog, and two cats. She dedicates this book to Bob and to Kelly, who loves a great mall.